LOCO FOR

LIZARDS

LOCO FOR LIZARDS

BY JIM CHERRY

NORTHLAND PUBLISHING

This book is dedicated to my father,
whose love of wit and words inspired my own.
—J. C.

ACKNOWLEDGMENTS

The author wishes to thank those whose contributions aided immeasurably to this volume: Ed Mell, Craig Ivani, Tara Teichgraeber, Melissa Kaplan, Patricka Fletcher, J. Webster, Michelle Savoy, David Knotter, Karla Olson, Jonathan O'Neill, and Dewey Webb.

COVER: Chameleon by Klaus Kranz. Petroglyph by Linda Kranz.
HALF-TITLE PAGE: Our postal service honors America's slowest moving lizard—a coincidence?
FRONTISPIECE: *Desert Disguise,* oil on canvas, by Ed Mell, 2000.

All photographs by Klaus Kranz, with the exception of pages 4, 6, 11, 12, 15, 26, 42, 43, 45, and 58.

Composed in the United States of America
Art Directors: David Jenney and Jennifer Schaber
Designers: David Jenney and Jennifer Schaber
Editor: Brad Melton
Production Editor: Karla Olson
Production Supervisor: Lisa Brownfield
Editorial Assistant: Kimberly Fox

Printed in Hong Kong by Midas Printing Limited

www.northlandpub.com

FIRST IMPRESSION
ISBN 0-87358-763-4
Library of Congress Catalog Card Number Pending

81/7.5M/7-00

CONTENTS

INTRODUCTION
THESE WILD THINGS

"It's better to be the head of a lizard than the tail of a lion."

GEORGE HERBERT

"Lizards? You want an entertaining book about lizards? I'm your man! Is there enough material? Are you kidding?"

I was in my publisher's office, trying to close the sale. I really wanted to write this book.

But immediately after scrawling across the dotted line, panic set in. "Lizards," I thought, "maybe he's right! How much interesting stuff can there be? What have I done?"

I slept little that night. The next morning I rose early and sped to the library. I spent the day buried in the musty-smelling stacks, browsing books on mythology, biology, anthropology, and herpetology. The more I read, the more "ologies" opened up. When the lights blinked, I staggered out to the parking lot, goofy with information overload.

I found, to my great relief, that lizards have insinuated themselves deeply into our culture, as stealthily as a hungry chameleon eyeing its prey. They drew me in. The more I learned about them, the more interested I became. After I did a few weeks research, friends begged me to stop talking about lizards. I couldn't help it. Fascinating facts abound, both about the creatures themselves and their every-where-at-once presence in cultures around the world.

Above: Coppery patina graces a cast-iron gecko. Below: A creation of skilled craftsmen passed on for generations. Just perfect for foot wipin'!

Left: Low-maintenance pets for those not overly charmed by "animation."

ST. GEORGE AND THE DRAGON, watercolor, by Tim Shields, 1998.

As for the creatures themselves, wild adaptations are common. There are lizards that fly, while others fast for months, walk on water, change colors, and run upside down on glass. There are species that camouflage themselves, vocalize, and expand their ears like bat wings. Their nonstop creative evolution may explain why they've outlived dinosaurs by sixty million years.

This means, of course, that lizards were here before mammals of any kind walked the earth, before Bob Hope, even before Strom Thurmond. Dinosaurs came and left while lizards went quietly about their lives. An ancient monitor lizard might have cocked his head to watch the last giant brontosaurus fall thunderously to wheeze his last breath.

Lizards much like the ones we see today were here, eating bugs and climbing trees, even before there were continents, when all the world's ground was one huge landmass. When the mass did separate, a few lizards went along for the ride on each chunk.

A carving of a horned lizard from Oaxaca, Mexico. Even his hot rod flame-job doesn't cheer up Mr. Frowny Face.

Compared to lizards, we humans are newcomers. They were crawling around here 340 million years ago. Modern *Homo sapiens* didn't rub together their first sticks until half a million years back. One has to wonder if they'll be here after we've gone?

Left: A horned liz to light your darkest night. Below: A tin, Mimbres-style wall hanging from Mexico.

Though I live in Arizona, a heaven for lizards, I'm a city guy and rarely encounter them. But, once I started this book, lizards ran across my path as I hiked, skittered off my porch, climbed up to my second floor window and peeked in as I sat writing, and once—I swear this is true—a gecko zipped up a wall beside us, stopped, and cocked his head to stare the very instant I mentioned this project to a friend.

Weird.

Were they egging me on? Lobbying for a positive portrayal? Impossible to say, but I did feel a growing empathy toward my subject, as if I had a responsibility to properly present them. But that came easily, as the more I learned, the greater my admiration grew. I came to see lizards' strangeness, which might put some off, as a beautiful expression of nature's mystery. These animals have survived longer than any other vertebrate by virtue of their astonishing adaptability. Since our planet seems to be rapidly shrinking to the size of a dorm room at an underfunded college, it makes sense for us to get to know our roommates a little better.

After all, is it really such a small thing that lizards enjoy the warmth of the same sun that we do, and walk the same rocky ground?

CHAPTER ONE
JUST THE FACTOIDS

"Hold fast the time! Guard it, watch over it, every hour, every minute! Unregarded it slips away, like a lizard, smooth, slippery, faithless, a pixy wife."

THOMAS MANN, *The Beloved Returns*, 1939

Left: Cast-pewter pin inspired by native Australians' rock-pecking art. Below: A gecko thermometer adopts the temperature of its surroundings just like the real thing!

PURE SCIENCE!

Scientists call lizards *Sauria* and pair them with snakes in the order Squamata. Lizards are set apart from their slithering cousins, however, by their legs and the fact that most lizards can blink, while snakes can't. So far, thirty-eight hundred species of lizards have been identified and grouped into eighteen families. Skinks, who share their name with a species found in the Sahara desert, are the largest group of lizards.

Lizards range all over the world, except for places where it gets too cold, because, despite all their amazing talents, heating themselves is one thing they haven't figured out how to do. Most U.S. varieties are found in the Southwest, with Arizona hosting forty-four species, the most of any state.

Name anything edible, and there's a lizard that eats it, from tiny jungle leaves to animals as large as deer. Lizards are the opposite of birds, who spend lavish amounts of energy to fly and thus need to eat constantly. Many species of lizards need little energy to crawl around, store fat in their tails, and can go for months without eating or drinking. Very efficient.

Of course, lizards are themselves a food source for other animals, such as birds, wild cats, javelinas, and snakes, sometimes with great specialization. According to *National Wildlife* magazine, during breeding season, the southwestern whiptail lizard accounts for 90 percent of the roadrunner's protein intake.

A rare glimpse of the mysterious Gila monster.
© 2000 by Larry Lindahl / Ty Lampie.

A lizard, most likely a whiptail, serves as dinner for a roadrunner. These birds' blinding speed runs burn huge amounts of energy. All too often the lizards aren't quick enough to prevent their becoming a perfect protein snack. Courtesy Bruce Berman.

Sizes of adult lizards range widely, from the tiny 1-and-1/4-inch-long dwarf gecko to the Komodo dragon, a ten-foot-long whopper straining the scales at three hundred pounds! He's a relative midget, as a check of the historical record reveals fossils of ancient lizards that grew thirty-four-feet long.

If you watch lizards, you'll notice they constantly flick their tongues. Lizards don't smell but instead taste the air with the Jacobson's organ, which sits in the roof of their mouths. Their tongues collect molecules from the air for instant analysis.

Lizards have a number of other wild tricks. Heliothermic lizards depend on the sun to raise their body temperature. Some, like the Gila monster, stick their heads out of their hiding places first, and heat up its small mass quickly. A special muscle constricts their jugular vein, slowing blood flow back to the body, much like a thermostat constricts coolant flow in a car in order to control temperature. This allows the blood to get extra warm before it flows back into the body.

Males of several species use brilliant color displays to attract mates, and defend their territory from other males. Some say Africa's true chameleons can change colors to match their surroundings and can even two-tone themselves, making half of their body brown to match a tree trunk and the other half green to match a leaf. Others are of the opinion that chameleons only change color according to temperature, light, and mood.

LOCO FOR LOCOMOTION

There's no stopping lizards; name a surface and there's a lizard who's found a way to run on it or through it. When it comes to mobility, there's a whole lot of adaptability goin' on!

Water lizards (which can reach three to four feet in length) have fringed toes that enable them to run across the surface of water. Saharan lizards have special feet so they can swim, but through sand, not water. Others, like collared lizards, do "wheelies," standing up on their hind limbs, much like certain dinosaurs are thought to have done. Geckos climb windows and walk on ceilings with thousands of special hairlike skin extensions on their foot pads, so tiny they're able to grip onto the smallest imperfections on the surface of glass. Their grip is so strong, that glass will break before they'll release. There's an oriental species called the draco that forgoes walking altogether, flying through the treetops supported by skin flaps on its flanks, stretched out on hugely elongated ribs. Monitor lizards (like the giant Komodo dragon) are the speed champs, running at ten miles per hour for short spurts to catch the small wild pigs they like for supper. Brazil's rain forest is home to a lizard that is too lazy to provide its own locomotion at all. The male Brazilian chameleon prefers to ride piggyback on its mate, fending off competitive suitors like a cavalry soldier.

Lizards who hang out in the open, away from the protection

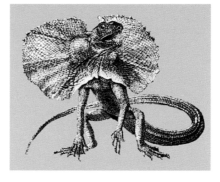

Left: Australian frill-necked in full display—scared?

of shrubbery, often have longer legs so they can run for safety faster. This is a disadvantage when traveling through dense brush; stumpier, ground-hugging species excel at traversing vegetation. The majority of desert-dwelling species have long legs to limit heat gain from the hot sands, often going so far as to extend their bodies to stand on their heels. The Southwest's collared and leopard lizards run extremely fast, using their hind legs only. Some compare their look while running to a mini T-Rex, which is not surprising since they're distantly related. In fact, dinosaur is derived from the Latin words *deinos* meaning "terrifying," and *sauros* or "lizard."

COMMUNICATION AND REPRODUCTION

Hand puppets— for those who'd prefer to let a lizard do their talking.

Geckos are the only lizards with the ability to vocalize; other species communicates with hisses, pushups, nips, color changes, and head bobs. Lizards do push-ups to warn off interlopers and bob their heads to attract mates.

It may well be that more complicated communication is unnecessary, as reproduction for lizards is, for the most part, a simple affair. In many species the male bites the female on the neck at the start of the mating process, a little love nibble. Most lizard species lay eggs, which they abandon, but some, like the blue-tailed skink, guard their nests and incubate their eggs. Others bear live young, and there's even a species that doesn't have its eggs fertilized by a male in order to reproduce.

LIZARD FAMILIES

There are eighteen lizard families, all with confusing Latin names, like Gekkonidae and Scincsidae. Instead of making your head spin with all the scientific details, I've chosen some facts about the most interesting lizard families. If you want comprehensive info, check out one of the books listed in the bibliography. For now, here are some highlights.

Gecko (Gekkonidae)
Africans came up with the name "gecko" from the sound the local species makes. Geckos like to hang out in human dwellings. But these cute little critters are no freeloaders; they earn their rent by eating bugs.

Skinks (Scincsidae)
Skink is the name of a small desert lizard that has generously given its name to the largest lizard family. They are capable of rapid color changes. Dried and powdered, they are eaten by Saharan desert dwellers who consider them a panacea for all kinds of ills and an aphrodisiac.

A skink.
"Sleek, ain't I?"

Chameleons (Chameleaontidae)
Opposable digits help chameleons grasp limbs to climb trees. They have amazingly sticky tongues that are as long as their bodies. They are lazy and slow, except for that ever-lovin' tongue, which they can whip out lightning fast to trap insects. These crusty critters can change color to match surroundings and swivel their eyes in different directions to look for meals or predators. They range in size from two inches to two feet. It's cute how they coil their tails up tightly when they are not using them.

I get a lot of compliments on my tail.

Iguana (Iguanidae)

Iguana grow up to six-feet long. They do "wheelies" when alarmed, standing up on their back legs and running. Not fast enough to prevent their capture, for they are a popular pet store item. They hang out in trees above water. When threatened, they drop into the stream or pond, where they can remain submerged for half an hour. They poke their eyes and noses out 'til the coast is clear, then climb back up on their perches. Unfortunately, jungle-dwelling humans have figured this out, so young boys shake their trees, then search for the iguanas in their watery hiding places. They are a valued source of protein for rain forest inhabitants. Males sometimes turn orange when they detect a female human in the midst of her menstrual cycle.

Anguis

Its only species, *A. Fragilis*, hangs out on grassy banks. Known in its native England as the "slow worm," it preys on slugs; it is one of the few animals (besides small humans with saltshakers) known to do so.

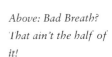

Monitors (Varanidae)

Monitors are the biggest lizards alive today; makes sense, they had ancestors who walked around amongst the dinosaurs. Today they're found in Africa, the Middle East, Asia, and Australia. Monitors are carnivorous with a vengeance, but they enjoy an occasional bite of fruit, turtle eggs, or fresh water mussels. The world's largest squamata is the Komodo Dragon, found on two tiny East Indian islands. You'd think they'd be frightening enough at ten-feet long, but they don't agree. When confronted, they inflate themselves, hiss violently, swing their tails around, and open their mouths in a threatening manner. Should all this fail, an African savanna monitor lizard has another trick: He rolls over on his back and plays dead. Since he runs at speeds of up to ten miles per hour, maybe he's just tired. Monitors don't worry if prey escapes; their mouths are so ripe with bacteria that their bite gives victims blood poisoning, killing them within a day or two.

Above: Bad Breath? That ain't the half of it!

Collared Lizards (Crotaphytus collaris)

Colorful southwestern beauties who like to bask on rocks out in the open, but make lightning quick getaways by rearing up to run superfast on their hind legs, maybe like dinosaurs did. If you're lucky enough to catch one, be careful; they have a real bite! Range from southeastern Utah to Missouri.

A turquoise collared lizard strikes a profile, showing off his smartly striped collar, detachable blue tail, and stylish chartreuse, white and aqua polka-dotted body banding. © 2000 by Larry Lindahl / Ty Lampie.

HORNED LIZARDS AND GILA MONSTERS

Shelves full of books have been dedicated to describing the characteristics of thousands of different lizard species. The limited space of this volume makes it impossible to do more than take a quick look at a couple of examples. I've chosen two that are prominent in the Southwest, where most of North America's varieties are found.

Horned Lizards (Phrynosoma)

If we're defined by what we do, it would be safe to call horned lizards defensive. In fact, with their array of six different strategies, they might also be called resourceful. First, horned lizards in different regions are effectively camouflaged with skin colors to match the local terrain,

Anybody see an anthill? Courtesy Randall D. Babb.

from reddish brown to dark gray. Second, horns on their sides give them a ragged, indistinct profile that makes them hard to spot. Those nasty-looking horns also make predators think twice about swallowing them. Snakes and birds who unwisely ignore the danger have been found with their throats punctured.

Third, since most of their predators don't eat carrion,

horned lizards often play dead when trapped. If that doesn't work, they go to defense number four, running as fast as they can, then suddenly freezing. A predator's eyes can't stop as fast as the lizard does and it often loses them against the background. This doesn't always work either, but the horny toad has two tricks left. Fifth, he can gulp air, inflating his body so much that he's bouncing on his belly with his legs off the ground. A hungry snake has to wonder if he's underestimated his prey's size. But, should even that fail, the lizard can unleash his sixth and ultimate trick: shoot foul-tasting blood out of his eyes at a range of up to four feet, frontwards or backwards! Understandably, this crimson splash usually discourages even the hungriest pursuer. Mexicans, impressed by these bloody tears, call horned lizards "sacred toads."

Since they like it hot, horned lizards flourish in the Southwest. On sunny desert mornings they can be found poking their heads up from their sand burrows then crawling out into the warmth of solar radiation. Exposing their broad, flat backs like a solar cell, they quickly get toasty. Very efficient, but, lacking the ability to cool themselves, they can easily overheat. This means they have to alternate between sun and shade throughout the day. Summer months find the horned ones scrambling around during mornings and late afternoons. They reverse this in winter, spending most of their time foraging midday, when the sun is at its warmest.

Once a horned lizard is sufficiently heated, he sets out in search of an anthill. Should he get lucky and find a moving column of his favorite insects, he quickly positions himself at its head and gobbles up the line. However, ants are made up mostly of an indigestible material called chitin, and they aren't all that nutritious. Thus, these lizards have to gobble massive quantities, two to five hundred mouthfuls each day, in order to get the nutrition they need. This requires a disproportionately large stomach mass, as much as 13 percent of their bodies. Their love of ants is an over-specialization that has hurt horned lizards in some areas, as the spread of inedible fire ants has led to a population decline.

Males defend their territory by rapidly bobbing their heads, which also serves as an introduction to other lizards. If the interloper does the same, the defender tries to get rid of him by doing push-ups. If this happens between a male and female during mating season, the courtship is highly abbreviated, forgoing dating, gifts, and proposals altogether. The male lizard quickly mounts the female's back, bites her neck, and hangs on as she saunters nonchalantly along, munching any insects that happen by.

Horny toads' armor does a good job of protecting them from predators, but humans have found a way to get control of them. Stroke the top of these lizards' heads and you will put them into a trance for up to ten minutes. Unfortunately, though horned lizards are sociable and seem to like human company, they make poor pets. They usually croak too soon, due to insufficient heat, and/or incorrect diet. Human development has led to the nonstop destruction of vast areas of horned lizard habitat. Their increasingly scarcity makes it a good idea to let them enjoy their wild lives.

*Silent Cal
and scaly pal.*

The Lizard that Met the President

One fine sunny day in 1897, the city fathers of Eastland County, Texas, held a public ceremony to dedicate a new courthouse. They had the cornerstone hollowed out to contain a time capsule. One of the officials spied his son nearby, playing with a horned lizard. On a whim the official threw the hapless lizard into the capsule. Thirty-one years later the county decided to build a new courthouse and unearthed the time capsule prior to demolishing the building. Curious about the lizard's fate, a large crowd gathered. When the cornerstone was lifted, a local reached in, recovered the dusty lizard and handed it over to a presiding official, whereupon it awoke, astonishing the multitude! No one ever publicly admitted to the switch and the ruse went undetected. The lizard was named Old Rip, toured the country to become a national celebrity, and was presented to President Calvin Coolidge in Washington, D.C.

Gila monsters' markings are like snowflakes—no two alike. © 2000 by Larry Lindahl / Ty Lampie.

Gila Monster (Heloderma Suspectum)

A whole section devoted to an underground, slow-motion reptile with skin like a beaded purse? Yes, because this is the mysterious Gila monster. He holds a number of records: America's only poisonous lizard, North America's largest species, and the slowest-moving lizard on our continent.

Adult Gila monsters average twenty-three inches long and weigh about three pounds. They are three to four inches long at birth and grow to full size within three years. They generally live for twenty years.

Their mysterious nature has inspired wild myths. Early settlers were convinced Gila monsters' bites were fatal.

It appears that Yearger had been fooling with a Gila monster, and in attempting to open the creature's mouth [he] was bitten on the right thumb. Instantly the poison took effect, and although every convenient remedy was applied he lived but a few hours.... This is the third or fourth death which has occurred in the Territory from bites of this reptile....

Cochise Record, Tombstone, Arizona Territory, MAY 2, 1884

Sounds convincing, but there's yet to be proven a case that wasn't actually due to a complication of other factors, usually alcohol, misguided post-bite care, or a pre-existing health problem.

If you ever see a Gila monster, you'd instantly understand how such a rumor got started. There's something primeval about them, lumbering along with their low-slung, slow-motion gate, strange, bumpy coat, and nasty-looking forked black tongue constantly flicking out to taste the air.

Gila monsters used to be called Aztec lizards by cowboys who invented all kinds of fanciful tales about the strange creatures.

> I jerked out my revolver and fired four shots at it but the balls all slipped off its tarnal hide back into the river and at last I got so mad I shook the pistol in the critter's face, and I'm a liar if it didn't jump at it and ketch the muzzle in its mouth, and what's more I couldn't git it away again. I pulled and jerked, and sweat and swore, but no use; and I believe mister lizard would hev pulled me plum into the river if I hadn't thought to cock the revolver and shoot it down his throat. The shot blew the body clean in two, and then I hope to die if the head and fore legs didn't get the pistol away from me, into the river and swim away with it.
>
> "The Gila Monster," *The (San Diego) World,*
> FEBRUARY 20, 1873

This isn't surprising, since the Gila monster is one of the least understood of animals. Maybe that's because they're antisocial, spending something like 96 percent of their time in underground burrows. So secretive are they, in fact, that a Gila monster nest has never been found, nor has one ever been observed hatching in its native habitat. These recluses usually emerge only in April or May, as the temperature's right then and there's lots of eggs and hatchlings for it to eat. The rest of the year? They store energy in their tails and live off it for months as they lay in a state of torpor deep underground.

Gila monsters feed on bird and reptile eggs, baby desert cottontail rabbits, squirrels, and other rodents, along with whatever lizards they can capture. Their wild-looking "beaded" coat is actually scales layered over tiny bits of bone, giving them an armor plating.

Late nineteenth century pioneers thought the Gila monster had no anus and that whatever it ate just putrefied as its digestive system completely absorbed its food. The theory was that this gave the monsters such bad breath that they could blow people away by breathing out a deadly black gas. This belief might have been inspired by Gila monsters' fierce hiss when threatened. Early settlers believed that a drop of its venom was poisonous enough to sterilize the ground for yards around.

Early in the twentieth century, Gila monsters were popular draws in carnivals and reptile gardens. Many were collected, sold, and shipped out of state. Because of concerns provoked by this commercial harvesting, in 1950 Arizona became the first state to pass a law protecting a poisonous reptile, banning the taking of either Gila monsters or horned toads without permission.

Though they conserve energy by moving slowly, when Gila monsters decide to strike they can lash out with shocking speed, clamping on their victims with the strength of a pit bull. They don't inject their venom neatly like snakes do; theirs is a much more primitive delivery system. Glands along the lower jaw produce poison that travels along grooves in their bottom teeth. Gila monsters simply lock down hard and chew in order to work their toxin into the flesh. Victims who've received serious bites describe extreme pain at the site of the wound followed by dizziness, nausea, and weakness for three to four days.

Though respectful of the lizard's ability to harm, Indians often think of them as also having healing qualities. The Seri Indians of Mexico's Sonoran coast heat the skin of Gila monsters and place it on their heads to cure headaches. Yaqui Indian healers place Gila monster skin over the problem area on a sick person's body in order to extract the poison that was causing illness.

LIZARD WORLD NEWS
Guaranteed—All these facts are

FIRST SPECIES TO CLONE ITSELF?

Though many colonies have been found, no males have ever been seen of some varieties of southwestern whiptail lizards. They all consist of females only. Scientists scratch their heads and say they must have worked out a reptilian version of cloning!

YOUR OLDEST RELATIVE A LIZARD?

"Lizzie the Lizard" was discovered in an abandoned limestone quarry near Bathgate, Scotland, in 1988. Dated at 340 million years old, she is the oldest known vertebrate, which makes her the earliest ancestor of reptiles, birds, and mammals like us!

Lizards Help Humans Live Longer

Human longevity researchers have found that lizards live longer when their core body temperature is lowered. Roy Walford, professor of pathology at the University of California Los Angeles, compared this phenomena to Indian yogis who lower the temperatures of their bodies through meditation and controlled breathing, perhaps accounting for their ability to live beyond a hundred!

LIZARDS—LIVING MOOD RINGS?

Lizards change their color as much to reflect emotional states as they do to camouflage themselves. You might say they express their emotions through color, just like the "mood rings" of a few years back—or like Rothko, that artist who painted color fields.

LIZARD PSYCHIC HOTLINE 1-800-LIZZARD

LIZARDS—A SUBSTITUTE FOR VIAGRA?

Saharan Africans make a popular aphrodisiac from the dried-out bodies of skinks that frequent their desert land.

Powdered skink is relied on by many northern Africans to rev up their sagging libidos!

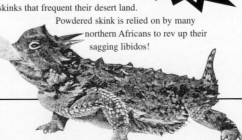

NEW VIAGRA SUBSTITUTE

GIRL AND LIZARD IN THREE-HOUR LIP LOCK!

Six-year-old Heather Ryland loved playing with the small lizards that hung around her family's yard in Corpus Christi, Texas. But one day she went too far and, overcome with a particularly cute little gecko on the garden wall, she brought it to her lips for a kiss. He locked onto her bottom lip and wouldn't let go! Heather ran screaming to her mother, but mom was too scared to help. Her brother James just laughed. Since there was nothing she could do, Heather resigned herself to walking around with a lizard attached to her lip. The lizard held his viselike grip for three hours before finally tiring and releasing his jaw.

LIZARD WALKS ON WATER!

Water lizards have specialized fringed toes that enable them to run across the surface of water like it's as hard and solid as a concrete sidewalk!

LIZARDS BORN WITH CAN OPENERS!

Lizards have a special "egg tooth" that they use like a throw-away can opener to rupture their eggshell at birth. Baby lizards shed it immediately after use.

EYES IN THE BACK OF THEIR HEADS!

Lizards have a special "third eye" underneath the skin at the top of their heads, which is sensitive to solar radiation.

STRANGE LIZARD SHATTERS LIKE GLASS—AND LIVES!

The amazing slender glass lizard, when threatened with capture, writhes and wriggles like a politician caught telling the truth, shaking off its tail or even shattering it into many tiny pieces like grandma's fine china!

AMAZING SELF-INFLATING LIZARD

In order to avoid becoming a meal for a predator, the southwestern chuckwalla flattens its body to slip into a crevice, then gulps air to inflate itself like a football, making it impossible to dislodge!

CHAPTER TWO
LIZARD CULTURE

A colorful, Mexican tin gecko to hang in your casa.

A lizard maiden was thirsty and crying.
A Gila monster ran up and was comforting her.
The lizard stopped, and then the Gila monster carried her off
And took her to wife.

TOHONO O'ODHAM SONG

Musicians, poets, filmmakers, photographers, painters, and sculptors have all found inspiration in *Sauria*, from rock 'n' rollers who identify with the wily crawlers, to filmmakers who use them to exploit audiences' fears, to painters inspired by their exotic beauty. Typically lizardlike, they crawled into our cultural lives so stealthily, few are even noticed.

LIZARDS IN MYTH

Given lizards' ubiquity, it isn't surprising that they pop up in myths and legends all over the world. Their universal success in adapting to wildly varied environments might have inspired those looking to explain humans' place in the grand scheme of things. At any rate, throughout history, they've played key roles in myths of all kinds.

Left page: COLLARED LIZARD AND SANTA RITA CACTUS, acrylic on canvas, by Anne Coe, 1994.

Australia

Deep in the outback of Australia, Aborigines have devised an ingenious means of keeping the peace between their tribes. They believe that each tribe is an exclusive keeper of a portion of the myths and songs of their people, thus each tribe is incomplete without the others. Various Aborigine tribes tell different tales of Lizard Men. Some say they brought about the first death when Kulu the Moon Man tried to rape the first women and the Lizard Men killed

him with a magic boomerang. Another tribe believes that the
Lizard Men gave ordinary men a way to contact departed ancestors. Yet another believes that they gave ancient Aborigine ancestors ceremonial instruments during the Dreamtime.

Another Aboriginal myth says Man was created in God's
image at the time of a great flood. Man felt lonely, so he cozied up
to the kangaroo, wombat, snake, and lizard, but found they lacked
sufficient presence of the Great Spirit. Finally, one night he awoke
to see Woman step out of a glowing tree. All the creatures danced
around, delighted. No doubt the man did a little jig himself.

Africa

Yoruba people of Nigeria believe that earth began as a boggy
marsh. Pretty boring. Ol-rum, the creator, decided things needed
firming up, so he sent a pigeon and a hen to scatter solid earth
over the world. After awhile, he got curious as to their progress
and sent a chameleon to inspect their work.

This myth is typical of those that African tribes tell of
slow-moving chameleons being involved in creation. Xhosa
and Zulu tribes believe God called the chameleon to the sky
and sent him to announce to men that, though they would
die, they would return to be born again. On his way he
met Kalulu the hare and relayed the message. Having heard
people mourning only the day before, Kalulu begged to be
allowed to speed the good news along. Though unsure, the
chameleon went along with Kalulu's plan, admonishing him
to remember the message clearly. Kalulu was a fast runner
with a poor memory, it seems, for the message he actually
delivered was "God says to you people 'Although you are suffering with life, you will also have death.'" By the time the
slow-poke chameleon showed up with a more accurate tran-
scription, it was too late. Kalulu's dark message had already
cast the shadow of death across the earth.

Another African myth concerns a chief who had a daughter
so beautiful that she was overwhelmed with suitors. The chief
decided to determine who would marry her with a hoeing contest. The suitor who could hoe the best would win her hand.
Hearing of this, the chameleon studied magic and ate medicines
to pump himself up for the contest. The day of the hoedown,

he waited until the other contestants were off digging their brains out, then he climbed on the hoe and sat back as it did the work itself! He just rode along as it flew past the other suitors sweating in the sun. The chameleon won decisively.

But the chief didn't want his daughter to marry a lizard, so he decreed a foot race to determine who would achieve groom status. Once again the clever chameleon came up with a scheme, turning into a needle and riding the tail of a rapid hartebeest. As the animal passed the chief's hut, the chameleon let go of the tail and was declared the winner by popular vote. The hartebeest started to weep. Legend has it that he has cried nonstop since that day, for, even today you can see what look like permanent tears in the loser's eyes.

Polynesia

Hawaiians tell of a man who was unable to feed his family so he went to a temple to discover a solution to his plight. The temple's god was Mo'or, which means lizard. (The only lizards known in the Hawaiian islands are small geckos that mostly hang around people's dwellings and catch insects.) The mighty Mo'o is a powerful god, who told the man he would die that night as the volcanic fires of Pele lit the clouds. But first he must give his wife burial directions. The man instructed his wife to bury his head near a freshwater spring, and his heart and entrails near the entrance to their house. He immediately dropped dead at her feet and his wife did as instructed. Then she went to sleep.

She awoke to find her house surrounded by thick vegetation. Where she'd buried her husband's heart there grew a bountiful tree surrounded by its fruit, which had fallen during the night. She named it (breadfruit) after her husband Ulu. A thicket of unknown plants bearing a strange long yellow fruit (bananas) clustered around the spring. The ground between her house and the spring was clogged with delicious sugar cane.

She fed her starving son. He immediately sprang back to health and grew to be a strong warrior, Mokoula, whose name graces an islet in Hilo Bay to this very day.

There was a brave resident of Maua named Ngaru, whose grandfather was Moko, the King of the Lizards. Due to her fair skin, his wife Tonga-tea was the envy of all the Mauans. Ngaru wished for fame and so decided to vanquish the greatest monsters of all: Tiko-kura, the storm wave; and Tumu-i-te-are-toka, the great shark. He procured the lightest surfboard he could find and cleverly named it Two, after the two monsters he was to battle. Then, Ngaru paddled out on his surfboard to fight the monsters as his grandfather, the great lizard Moko, shouted warnings from the shore. Finally, after eight days of battle, Ngaru threw his surfboard to the evil spirits who returned to their home in the depths with great relief.

Unfortunately, prolonged exposure to the sun and sea had turned Ngaru's skin quite dark and, seeing this, his fair-skinned wife Tong-tea rejected him. Moko the Lizard King then instructed Ngaru to bury himself in a fern-lined hole, which he did, emerging on the eighth day so fair that lightning seem to flash from his skin. His wife Tonga-Tea refused to believe it was him, but once convinced, begged him to return to her. Ngaru, still smarting from her rejection said, "Never will I return to thee."
Despairing, Tonga-tea chewed a poisonous plant and expired.

Early Christians

Early Christians believed that when a lizard grew old and its eyesight began to fail, it would wedge itself into a wall as night fell with its face pointed due east. As the morning sun rose it would burn away cloudiness from the lizard's eyesight, restoring it. Christians used this as a metaphor of renewing one's life through a reaquaintance with the light of faith.

Native American

Though tribes have differing beliefs, many Native Americans consider lizards to be powerful beings. For instance, Navajos consider the Gila monster the original medicine man. To promote healing, Yaqui Indians place pieces of Gila monster hide on affected parts of the body. Apaches consider the sighting of a Gila monster as a sign of approaching rain.

NO–PA'H–NO–MAH, THE LONG–TIME–ALONE–BOY, *by Maynard Dixon, 1923.*

"If you should desire news of me, go ask the little horned toad, whose home is in the dust."

—MAYNARD DIXON

There's a Tohono O'odham legend that offers an explanation for how the Gila monster got its unique beaded skin. All the desert critters had been invited to the first saguaro wine festival. The Gila monster made itself a special coat of colorful desert rocks. It was a big hit at the party. The lizard decided then and there to wear it for all time.

Tohono O'odham Indians of Arizona also ascribe great powers to horned lizards, believing they have the power to affect the course of a person's life, to make them sick and heal them.

Navajos tell of a lizard who ran up a sunflower stalk to escape from a coyote. The coyote could have easily knocked the stalk down and captured him, so the lizard said, "Look, I am holding up the sky." The atmosphere was stormy and turbulent, so he added, "You must help by keeping your eyes on the heavens. Look! Look up!" He waited until the coyote grew weary and dizzy, then the lizard climbed down and escaped. The coyote realized he'd been had and so resolved, "These other animals are too clever for me, I will never listen to them again!"

Christine McHorse, LIZARD POT, pit-fired micaceous clay and piñon pitch, 1990. Courtesy Chuck and Jan Rosenak.

ATTACK OF THE MUTANTS WITH INCOMING MISSILES, acrylic on canvas, 1987.
Courtesy Anne Coe.

LIZARDS IN ART

Since lizards have skittered into every nook and cranny of
human culture, it isn't surprising that the art world is no exception. What is it about them that inspires artists? Though herps
have appeared on rock drawings, paintings, carvings, and sculp-
tures in cultures all over the world, going back very far in time,
their presence in art seems as mysterious as the creatures themselves. Ancient, so-called "primitive" artists' thinking about their
subject matter is lost and most contemporary artists prefer to let
the work do the talking.

Often, lizards fill the same role in art as they do in nature:
modest little creatures skittering around in the background, as in
Hieronymous Bosch's well-known painting, *Garden of Earthly
Delights.* M.C. Escher utilized lizards in several pieces to drama-
tize his graphic depictions of optical conundrums, but, his
explanation of why is as puzzling as his work, "I have never
done any work with the aim of symbolizing a particular idea,
but the fact that a symbol is discovered or remarked upon is

GARDEN OF EARTHLY
DELIGHTS, *detail
from, oil on canvas,
by Hieronymus
Bosch, 1500.*

valuable to me . . ." Contemporary artists
such as Anne Coe and Tim Shields are more
likely to paint them as featured stars in surreal
tableaux. If it's true that a picture is worth a
thousand words, maybe it's also true that to
explain art is to destroy its magic—at least it
provides an excuse for keeping this brief.

LIZARDS IN ADVERTISING

Never above exploiting the public's affections,
ad agencies have cast lizards in all manner of
print ads, commericals, and packaging
designs. Iguanas, geckos, and their cousins
have been pressed into service, flogging a fat
list of goods and services including: insurance,
cellular telephones, beer, convenience stores,
CD recorders, and bottled juices.

Budweiser's lizards are the best known of
all. The beautifully animated chameleons,
Frank and Louie, star in an extremely popular
series of television commercials. Their imagi-
natively written scripts developed herpsonali-
ties that delighted viewers. Other ad lizards
include wild, baseball-capped, dune-buggy
driving desert lizards used by a convenience
store chain to promote mega-gulp soft drinks.
A cell phone maker used print ads that drew a
parallel between a mutable-colored lizard and
switchable color faceplates. Geico insurance
company employed a friendly gecko to personalize its services.
The trend amongst marketers to use animal mascots to "friendly
up" products has given *Sauria* a greatly increased visibility.

As ad agencies are paid for their savvy use of imagery to
attract customers, their deployment of geckos and iguanas may
be a sign that Americans are, at last, warming to the charms
of lizards.

LIZARDS ON FILM, OR SOMEBODY ALWAYS SHOOTS THE LIZARD

With millions of dollars at stake, Hollywood movie makers take great pains to reflect ticket buyers' views. If you wonder what people think about a subject, check out how it's shown onscreen. Lizards' movie roles are a perfect example. They rarely appear, but when they do it's usually as unsympathetic, and thus disposable, creatures or as monstrous bad guys who are used to frighten characters and/or the audience. More often than not, they're quickly blown away as punishment.

Butch Cassidy and the Sundance Kid (**1969**)

Halfway through the movie Butch and the Kid are on the lam in the trackless wastes. Their nerves are on edge as they scan a dead quiet, panoramic landscape. Suddenly there's a scratching sound behind them. Without pausing to look, Sundance swivels and shoots with cowboy lightning quickness and a Gila monster tumbles down the cliff face, leaving a trail of blood.

The Freshman (**1990**)

A Komodo dragon hatches while opening credits roll in this comedy starring Marlon Brando and Matthew Broderick. Broderick's character is hired to deliver a six-foot Komodo dragon for mobster Brando (doing a turn on his Godfather character). The reptilian thespian holds his own in several scenes, even opposite the mighty Marlon, who's founded a highly profitable "gourmet club" specializing in endangered animals. The Komodo appears to be headed for the stewpot. But after a number of convoluted plot twists, the movie ends with Broderick and Brando walking through a cornfield into the sunset, together with the lizard.

Matthew Broderick as Clark Kellogg proves the importance of leash laws as he walks his scaly costar in Andrew Bergman's THE FRESHMAN *(TriStar, 1990). Courtesy Photofest.*

A pregnant Godzilla chooses Manhattan as her nest site in Ronald Emmerich's GODZILLA
(TriStar / Independent, 1998). Courtesy Photofest.

Godzilla

With sixteen starring roles since his 1956 debut, Godzilla is easily
the best-known cinematic lizard of all. My personal favorite,
Godzilla vs. the Smog Monster (1972), was a blatant attempt to
win our sympathy by pitting the big galoot against an eco-creep
born of air pollution. But all too soon, catalytic converters and
emission inspections made even this a hollow victory. Sometimes
even a giant lizard can't win.

The Giant Gila Monster (1959)

"Only Hell could breed such an enormous beast, Only God
could destroy it!" A lead role at last for the much maligned Gila
monster but, of course, he's the bad guy. In this forgotten classic a
titanic atomic mutant Gila monster whups up trouble in a southwestern trailer court. The beaded behemoth goes too far and the
world is saved by a hero teen who blows him up by driving a
nitroglycerin-packed hotrod into his giant beaded-monster gut!
     Thanks, kid!

One Million B.C. (1940)

A black-and-white classic starring lizards with glued-on cardboard fins acting as dinosaurs. Victor Mature does a courageous job, battling a variety of sham-a-saurs with just his wits, a stick, and his pompadour.

The color remake, released in 1966, is an overheated caveman glam-slam starring Neanderthal knockout Raquel Welch in a fur bikini.

Cavemen battle a fierce sham-a-saur in Hal Roach's ONE MILLION B.C. *(UA, 1940). "If we bring this one down we'll have leftovers for weeks!"*

Courtesy Photofest.

The Parent Trap (1998)

Amazing—a remake that equals, if not surpasses, a classic original. These filmmakers got it so right, they even expanded the lizard's role! This time, after the fun with the water bottle, identical twin Annie (or is it Hallie?) perches the lizard smack dab atop the meticulously groomed head of dad's fat-free fiancé Meredith. She freaks and grabs for it. The lizard freaks and tries to escape by crawling down her face and into the first dark hole it can find—her gaping mouth! As Annie says when she thinks up her scheme for terrorizing the hapless gold digger: "Brilliant!"

Assorted adventurers follow an explorer's trail down an extinct Icelandic volcano and fight off dinosaur imposters in Henry Levin's JOURNEY TO THE CENTER OF THE EARTH *(20th-Fox, 1959). Courtesy Photofest.*

"I am the lizard king. I can do anything!"
— JIM MORRISON

Journey to the Center of the Earth (1959)

Multi-talent Pat Boone took a break from recording watered down versions of rhythm-and-blues hits to try his hand at acting in this Technicolor adaptation of the Jules Verne classic. The squeaky clean one plays an explorer driving a bizarre Victorian boring machine deep into the earth. Somewhere just north of magma-ville, he and his brave band encounter a giant lizard and have quite a set-to before escaping in their dry-land submarine, allowing Pat to return to the surface for a future of receding record sales and hairline.

The Doors (1991)

Lead singer/songwriter Jim Morrison's identification with lizards is symbolized by an early shot of Jim hitchhiking out in the desert. A close-up profile of a lizard sets an ominous tone. Later, along with his new band mates, Morrison visits the desert on some kind of drug-fueled spiritual bonding quest and the lizard pops up again.

Freaky scene, man!

Treasure of the Sierra Madre (**1948**)
Fred Dobbs (Humphrey Bogart) doesn't believe his gold-digging
partner Curtin (Tim Holt) when he tells him he's after a Gila
monster under the rock where Dobbs has stashed his gold. When
Curtin dares him to reach down there and see for himself, Dobbs
refuses. They scrap and Curtin shoots the lizard.

Somebody always shoots the lizard.

ROCKIN' SQUAMATA!

Rock and roll might be the last place you'd expect lizards to turn
up, but think again. Lizards' penetration of "beat" music is as
deep as the bass notes on a James Brown funk track. There's
bands with lizard names, references in lyrics, even rock festivals
named after the splay-legged ones.

The American South, where rock and roll was born, has a
long tradition of calling it the "devil's music." Since the devil is
often depicted as reptillian, maybe there's a connection. Robert
Johnson is commonly considered the greatest of the original
bluesmen who laid down the roots of rock and roll. He's said to
have met the devil at the crossroads where he sold his soul in
exchange for an unearthly helping of talent, but, as Robert
was also said to have greatly enjoyed distilled beverages, it
might have been a passing horny toad.

*Hard rockers Saigon
Kick invite you to "Do
the Lizard!"*

Some bands with lizard names include: The
Lounge Lizards; Thundering Lizards; Aberdeen
Lizards; The Flying Lizards; Lizard Train;
Lizard's Convention; Lizard Music; Austin
Lounge Lizards; Big Lizard; Leapin' Lizards;
The Jesus Lizard; Sammy, Elwood, and the
Lounge Lizards; The Geckos; Big Nick & the
Gila Monsters; and The Fancy Lizards.

Lizard Songs
On The Doors' *Absolutely Live* there's a six-song set grouped
under the title "Celebration of the Lizard." It starts with a lyric
about some character waking up in a strange hotel with a snake
beside him. Arcane reference-lover Morrison launches into a

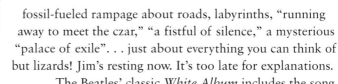

Illustration by the author.

fossil-fueled rampage about roads, labyrinths, "running away to meet the czar," "a fistful of silence," a mysterious "palace of exile". . . just about everything you can think of but lizards! Jim's resting now. It's too late for explanations.

The Beatles' classic *White Album* includes the song "Happiness Is a Warm Gun." The credit reads McCartney/Lennon, but it's an obvious Lennon pen-job. John raga-whines surreal imagery, including a line about "a lizard on a window pane." That would be a gecko, Johnny.

David Bowie's bleakly futuristic 1974 album *Diamond Dogs* has a song, "Rock and Roll with Me," with this oblique lyric: "I always wanted new surroundings / A room to rent while the lizards lay crying in the heat." Nice to have a place to lay one's head at such times!

Billy Corgan, leader of the Smashing Pumpkins, composed "Lizards," a moody instrumental song, for the soundtrack of the movie *Ransom* (1996). But Billy didn't stop there. He also produced and played all the instruments except drums. Then he shaved his head again.

Post-modern musical jester Beck Hansen's funkadelic soul-strut song cycle, *Midnite Vultures,* includes a song, "Pressure Zone," with the chorus, "Lizards in the pressure zone / Mother knows it's only a phase." Creative chameleon that he is, Beck knows about phases.

Long-haired, pierced-nose rockers Saigon Kick released an album entitled *The Lizard* in 1992. Its snappy title song's lyric commands listeners to dance, "When I tell you people to do the lizard / Pull yourself together and take a listen." Unfortunately, few lent an ear, and "The Lizard" failed to catch on as a teen boogie sensation.

Other Rock and Roll/Lizard Connections

Lizard '99 Festival was a week long "rockfest" held in scenic, coastal Cornwall, England, near an ancient Stonehenge-like rock pile. It featured Kula Shaker and James, along with more primi-cool rhythm makers like the drummers of Burundi.

Iggy Pop, nee James Osterberg, got his start pounding drums for a band called The Iguanas. His bandmates started calling him Iggy to ridicule him, but Iggy went on to a decades-long career as one of the most influential rock artists, and we never heard of the Iguanas again. So there!

LIZARDS ON THE WEB

Anyone who's curious about lizards' penetration of our culture might want to spend some time surfing the Web. My favorite search engine lists 84,390 Web sites relating to *sauria*, 957 for Gila monsters alone. It's wild to see how far a simple word like "lizards" can take you. There's the expected sites for pet fanciers and general fans of herps (Lizards! Lizards! Lizards!.com) to one chronicling the hard partyin' lifestyles of Harley riding bikers (lizards-lounge.com) to a site for ever-faithful Duran Duran fans called The Lizard King (http://lizardking.simplenet.com). (I asked its Webmaster why it was called that and he replied, "I just liked it. Besides, Jim Morrison called himself the Lizard King." Yeah, yeah. We know!)

I spent too much time on a site for a beautiful South Pacific paradise, Lizard Island, which lies twenty-seven miles off the coast of Queensland, Australia. It's home to a skittle of monitor lizards. (www.austresorts.com.au/lizard.htm)

Save Our Lizards and Snakes (www.ritch.net/sols/) advocates protection laws in Nevada, which, unlike California, Arizona, and New Mexico, gambles with the fate of its reptiles by failing to prohibit their capture and sale.

Cyberlizards (www.nafcon.dircon.co.uk/index.html) includes descriptions of various species and their suitability as pets, along with advice on caring for lizards, pages on rock and roll, cult TV, and computer games.

Busweiser's scheming lizards, Frank and Louie, have 615 Web sites listed on one search engine I checked, demonstrating television's awesome power to boost even animated chameleons to superstar status.

On the Web, any subject like this splits fractally, and changes every day. After all, it's the Internet. We can't guarantee that these sites will be there when you take a look, but you might enjoy doing your own search and surf. We can guarantee that there is a whole lot of information out there.

CHAPTER THREE

GABBIN' WITH A GECKO:
AN EXCLUSIVE INTERVIEW

Godzilla's foot crushes a fifty-story building like so many match-sticks. He gloats by breathing fire that burns down an airport. Really bad guy, or just misunderstood? Actually, he's typical of the way we exploit lizards. If we aren't watching them destroy Tokyo, we're slipping into a pair of boots made from their hides. Is it any wonder lizards are angry?

And yet, stoic creatures that they are, not one has crawled forward to explain the lizards' point of view.

Until now.

While researching this book I came home late one night to find a little gecko hanging around my porch light. "I'm writing a book about your kind," I said to him. "Mind if I study you?"

I don't expect you to believe it, dear reader, but I swear the little guy bobbed his head in response! Little could I have known what a spiral into madness that innocent motion was to inspire.

For weeks he showed up each night and I studied the gecko's every movement, struck by a growing sense that the little fellow really was trying to chat in some bizarre way. Eventually his trust must have grown, for he began coming inside and hanging around my ceiling light. Since this meant a tougher hustle for his nightly insect meal, I figured there had to be a reason. "Maybe," I thought, "he really is trying to communicate with me!"

I stared at the gecko fixedly, droning on endlessly about this and that, but nothing seemed to be getting through. I decided to stay up all night, a ball point pen and a legal tablet on my lap, a pot of strong coffee by the side of my comfortable armchair. I meticulously noted his pattern of head bobs and squeaks, con-centrating til my head hurt, trying in vain to make sense of it all.

Left page: Thirty years after the original monster's rampage, a new Godzilla emerges and attacks Japan in Koji Hashimoto and R. J. Kizer's GODZILLA 1985 *(New World Pictures, 1984). Maybe he's angry at the lack of Big & Tall shops in downtown Tokyo. Courtesy Photofest.*

By early morning I was dead tired, red eyed, and discouraged, like some obsessive nut in an Edgar Allen Poe story.

I finally collapsed as the sun came up. Depressed and exhausted, wondering if I was losing my mind, I turned in early the next evening. As I lay in bed, unable to sleep, staring up at nothing, the little gecko skittered out into a ray of cool blue moonlight shafting across my ceiling and head-bobbed his customary "Hello!"

Suddenly, call it divine inspiration, a sleep-deprived imagination, or the ravings of a mind unhinged by an unholy obsession, but in a sudden blinding flash I intuited the reptile's strange code! I could read his squeaks, blinks, tongue flicks, and body movements like a book! In a short time I was able to decipher entire phrases, and thus transcribe the dialogue I present here.

Of course, dear reader, I can't expect you to believe my strange tale, but shouldn't anyone who's spent happy moments speaking to their dog or cat at least give me the benefit of the doubt?

J: Why have you decided to speak to us now?

G: If you've spent time in our habitats, you've noticed we  geckos enjoy your company. We see a lot, hanging around on your ceilings. Not me, personally, but some lizards think you humans are a bit self-absorbed. Maybe it's time you got to know more about us.

J: Why do you say we're self-absorbed?

G: Well, you really don't seem interested in us beyond making monster lizard movies or staring at us in glass boxes at the zoo. I don't know, maybe it's the cold-blooded thing; you think that means we don't have feelings, too?

J: Well, warm bloodedness has advantages over cold bloodedness . . .

G: Not "cold-blooded," please! We lizards consider that a put-down. The proper term is "ectothermic." Anyway, so you can heat and cool your bodies . . . big deal! We're actually more in tune with our surroundings, at least temperature-wise. Anyway, we're not actually cold-blooded. Our body temperatures are about the same as yours. It's just much more efficient, energywise, to get your warmth from your surroundings than burn up calories heating yourself. Not to mention all the money we save on wool sweaters and deodorant. Anyway, if you're so good at regulating your body temperature, what's with all the heating and air-conditioning?

J: Not to brag, but we humans do have larger, more complex brains . . .

G: Okay, we have simpler nervous systems, but guess what . . . that means we don't have to think about taxes, flossing, or programming VCRs! Besides, if you think you're so clever, try changing your skin color to match your surroundings some time.

J: What's a typical day like for you, Mr. Gecko?

G: Night, not day. We geckos don't start swinging til the sun goes down. Anyway . . . I, uh, wake up under a rock, or sometimes I sleep in a crack in the wall. Takes me a minute or two to come up to speed. When I feel revved I get busy looking for a meal.

J: What's your favorite meal?

G: Bugs. I like bugs pretty much. I climb up onto somebody's ceiling, eat a buncha bugs, then I climb down and hide under a rock. The next night I go back and hang around the ceiling again. Pretty routine deal. Boring, actually! The thing those idiot bugs have for lights! But it's easy pickin's, and the light bulbs help keep me warm, too. Anyway, at least I ain't a snake.

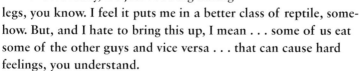

J: Do you resent snakes?

G: Not really, it's just . . . I dig having legs, you know. I feel it puts me in a better class of reptile, somehow. But, and I hate to bring this up, I mean . . . some of us eat some of the other guys and vice versa . . . that can cause hard feelings, you understand.

J: We have a pride of lions, a gaggle of geese, a herd of cattle, but what about you lizards? I propose the term a "skittle of lizards," referring to your characteristic running gate.

G: Whatever, but, truth be told, we lizards are pretty much

loners. You won't see us forming bowling teams or mobbing up to attend conventions so we can get drunk and wear silly hats.

J: How do you feel about all the merchandise that's been produced with your image?

G: In contrast to the howling coyote, chihuahua, and  kokopelli fads, we lizards have much less merchandise out there. We're happy building slowly, creating a more tasteful line. Lizard-embellished goods have been around since the stone age. That's no accident, my friend—that's good brand management.

J: Seen any of the Godzilla movies?

G: Yeah, I've caught a couple on TV. Of course, crawling around on ceilings means I watch upside down, so I might not be givin' Godzilla a fair chance, but—you call that a lizard? Isn't it actually a sweaty guy in a rubber suit?

J: But you are related . . .

G: Okay, so we're related, doesn't everyone have a troubled cousin or two somewhere in their family tree? I worry about the representation though; you have to admit, we lizards have actually been quite harmless to you humans.

J: For the most part, but you have to admit Gila monsters have a nasty bite!

G: Those beaded bad boys have a nasty rep, but personally, I've never had a problem with them. You leave them alone, they won't mess with you, that's what I think. Of course that's easy for me, since we geckos like climbing on ceilings and they spend nearly their whole lives underground. They do pack a poisonous venom, but, calling them monsters . . . no wonder they're cranky!

J: Anything you think we humans could learn from you lizards?

G: Well, for one thing, you've never seen a fat lizard . . . some of you humans might try laying off the french fries!

J: We humans portray the devil as lizardlike. Does that bother you?

G: Oh, that's been a sore point for millennia. Don't know how it got started, but two can play that game. We say he has nose hair and wears polo shirts!

J: You've heard the derogatory term, Lounge Lizard?

G: Sometimes I wonder if you humans are deliberately trying to insult us. I mean, when's the last time you saw a lizard sip a dry martini? Or take a drag off a Lucky as he tries to pick up a blonde? Seems like all-too-human behavior to me.

J: Please excuse me for pointing this out, but you seem a little testy today . . .

G: Hey! I'm molting here, okay? You ever molt? I thought not.

J: Any other resentments that your species has against ours?

G: Three words—handbags, boots, belts!

TOP TEN THINGS HUMANS CAN LEARN FROM LIZARDS

10. Change your skin color, not your clothes. No more laundry!
9. Grocery stores unnecessary if you have long tongues that move really fast.
8. Aging not a problem if you're born wrinkly.
7. Looking for an effective weight loss diet? Try three squares a day of gnats and fly larvae.
6. Lay in the sun all day. Never need sunscreen!
5. Ability to camouflage oneself helpful when goofing off at work.
4. Stop exterminating insects. Start eating them!
3. Tired of mortgage payments and property taxes? Try living under a rock.
2. Lay eggs. Save on maternity clothes!
1. Tails are easily detachable. Try that with your butt!

CHAPTER FOUR

LIZARD LOVERS SPEAK!

Lovers of *sauria* come in all degrees, from kids who trap a horny toad in a cigar box to scientists who dedicate entire careers to studying them. Some, such as our interview subjects, make lizards their life's work. Melissa Kaplan freely dispenses copious amounts of information about herps through her Web site while caring for an unending parade of troubled lizards at home. Herpetologist Craig Ivani tends the Arizona–Sonora Desert Museum's collection and specializes in the study of the activities of accidentally introduced species.

MELISSA KAPLAN, LIZARD EXPERT

Have a question about lizards? You might ask a veterinarian, but if he or she can't help, perhaps you'd call a herpetologist. But if even that fails, you might contact the person they call. Self-taught super-expert Melissa Kaplan fills in the blanks on her metic-

Lizard hijinks make Melissa Kaplan smile.

ulously researched Web site (http://anapsid.org/) where you can research to your heart's content for free. Kaplan blends her natural sensitivity to animals with a disciplined approach to info-mongering.

Kaplan's activities are a labor of love, but it wasn't always so. For years she spent five days a week laboring diligently under the fluorescent lights of a corporate cubicle world, dreaming of what she'd rather be doing. Then, suddenly, her company down-sized, bought out her contract, and freed her. This thrilled Kaplan. Finally, she could do what she'd always wanted and join a crew rescuing animals wounded in environmental disasters. Given her first job assignment—to clean birds injured in an oil spill—Kaplan joyfully set to work in a poorly ventilated,

Left: Handsome collared lizard couple—an "item" or "just friends?"
© 2000 by Larry Lindahl / Ty Lampie.

foul-smelling hangar, scrubbing crude oil off sick and dying birds. Engrossed in her efforts, she failed to notice that sixteen-hour shifts in a room filled with toxic fumes were affecting her health. In a cruel demonstration of the adage "no good deed shall go unpunished," Kaplan became disabled when excessive exposure to petro-chemical toxins led to a severe neuro-immune endocrine collapse. She became allergic to birds, animals, and a host of other common things.

But she discovered that she wasn't allergic to reptiles.

"I got an iguana and immediately ran into problems with his diet and behavior. Researching cures made me knowledgeable enough that others began asking questions. I printed up a one-page care sheet and distributed it to other lizard owners. One page became two, two became ten, then twenty-five. It got expensive and unmanageable. I plugged in a modem and started posting answers to questions people had on the Internet. That led me to establishing my own Web site. My career's evolution has been driven by the information explosion.

"I've been disabled for the last ten years, so I've had time to devote to this. Since I'm too ill to work on animal rescue, I can do the most good on the Web.

"I like lizards because they can be read. Though they're harder to read than mammals, they can be understood. I enjoy making the connection with an animal, where there's a spark of understanding and they communicate with you. I try to communicate on their terms rather than ours, which is very different. They're still wild animals and look at the world that way. We need to see how they see things."

Getting to understand them on their level has enabled Kaplan to work miracles with troubled lizards. Her sensitivity has proven beneficial both to animals and their owners. "People bring me difficult iguanas to see if I can do anything with them. When the lizards hiss at me, I hiss back. They try biting, rolling around, lashing their tails, but when all their tricks fail, their eyes get wide. They realize they can't push this human around and they get past the fight for dominance."

"Lizards can train us," she says. "Iguanas in particular like to dominate. Someone will bring me a baby iguana. As they try to hold him, he'll thrash around, thinking he's about to be eaten.

If you put him down, he learns to thrash around in order to be released, but if you hold on until he settles, he learns it's your decision and that staying calm means he'll be put down. Then, once he learns to relax, I try grooming and petting him. Soon he learns it's pleasurable and relaxes to enjoy it."

Kaplan says people interested in a lizard pet would do well to consider acquiring a bearded dragon. "They have an innate curiosity. They're friendly, inquisitive, and don't need to be tamed like an iguana. And, unlike iguanas, they understand that a vacuum cleaner won't eat them."

Kaplan likes living with her reptilian charges. She enjoys providing them with a happy, healthy environment. "I like to let them roam freely through the house. They need stimulation, because captivity is stressful for them."

She recommends other species as being relatively easy to keep as well. "Leopard geckos, fat-tailed geckos, and, though harder to find for sale, Australia's blue-tongued skinks are great. My blue-tongued is named Sluggo. I take him to lunch with friends and he's the center of attention. He likes to be handled."

I asked her why she likes lizards so much. "What's not to like?" she replied. "They're very talented, responsive, companionable creatures. They even get jealous if I spend too much time with one or the other!"

HANGIN' WITH A HERPETOLOGIST

The Arizona–Sonora Desert Museum is a combination zoo, botanical garden, and natural history museum located near Tucson, Arizona. Two miles of paths take visitors through 21 acres of beautiful desert, where they see a collection of over 300 animal species and 1200 kinds of plants. Its natural, isolated setting makes for a truly "real" experience of southwest wildlife. I was fortunate to have a private tour conducted by Craig Ivani, whose card reads: Collections Manager Herpetology.

Don't try this at home! Herpetologist Craig Ivani handles a venomous Mexican beaded lizard. Photo by the author.

Craig Ivani never wondered what would happen if a really big lizard, far larger than any native species, got loose to roam the wilds of Arizona. These are things even a herpetologist would rather not find out. But he says, "Spiny-tailed iguanas proved to be wily enough to get loose, officially achieving 'introduced species' status when enough individuals escaped their cages at Arizona–Sonora Desert Museum to establish a breeding colony. Fake rock formations built to house species like horned mountain sheep are perfect simulations of the terrain these big lizards like in central and northern Mexico. The museum grounds provide lots of green plants to eat and warm rocks to heat them up." Happiness, if you're a spiny-tailed iguana.

Ivani has worked at the Arizona–Sonora Desert Museum since the mid-eighties. Unlike most herpetologists, Ivani didn't have a youthful fascination with lizards. "My curiosity began when I studied reptiles as an undergraduate volunteer here. My biggest interest has been with the spiny-tailed iguana, introduced in the early seventies as a captive animal. We felt it was important to see if they're spreading off the museum grounds and, if so, what kind of impact they're having. It's an interesting animal. So far, we're not seeing any convincing proof that they've spread off-site."

I ask him about the place of Arizona–Sonora Desert Museum in comparison to other zoos with lizards. "Of course, we do have a strong regional focus and are most unusual in that we're located in the middle of the desert. We're not in the middle of a city trying to convince visitors they're in a natural habitat."

The museum's funding comes from gate receipts, donations, and membership fees, Ivani says. "It's a private, not-for-profit institution that's been here since 1952. Our international reputation gives us a huge base of people to hire from. On my staff we have people from all over the U.S. and one from Canada. I'm the only local."

I ask him why Arizona has the most lizard species of any state. "Arizona has the most species because, first of all, it's in the South, which makes it good place for ectothermic, or so-called cold-blooded animals. It has a good variety of habitats, from low desert to ten thousand-foot-tall peaks. It has lots of

rocky areas, which lizards like. Also there's an abundant supply
of insects for lizards to feed on. The Sonoran Desert has two
rainy seasons, which give it eleven inches of rain. This is actually
an inch over the technical cut-off point for deserts, making for a
very lush one, filled with stuff lizards like to eat.

"In urban situations, one of the most common lizards is an
introduced species, the Mediterranean house gecko, which ranges
all across the southern U.S. Any lizards that you see hanging
around walls or your porch light are the Mediterranean house
gecko. Other species you'll see in town are the western whiptails.
If you have natural habitat, you'll probably find them, along with
desert spiny lizards, and the occasional regal horned lizard."

Are there any southwestern lizards in danger of extinction?

"The flat-tailed horned lizard from the southwest corner of
Arizona is suffering from a lot of damage from all-terrain vehi-
cles, but so far has not been listed as endangered. Arizona has so
much of its land designated as military bases, reservations, and
parks. This has a secondary effect of providing lizards with
unspoiled habitats."

What good is the study of lizards to the average person?

"We have lot of people who call us and say 'I have all these bugs
I'm trying to get rid of . . .' We're trying all these pesticides, and
they don't work for long. The chemicals seep into the water table.
The pesticides kill lizards' food and kill them, too. If you say
'I'm not going to tolerate having spiders, crickets etc. running
around inside, but I'm going to allow them outside,' then you
allow those lizards and toads and so forth that naturally take
care of those problems to do their job and you avoid the use of
chemicals and their secondary effects. With insecticides you're
actually fighting the very thing that's trying to help you elimi-
nate pests."

Why is it that some people can't relate to lizards?

"People are prejudiced against other people with different skin colors, so it shouldn't be surprising that they can't relate to something that has scales, is cold-blooded, and lacks a voice. Sometimes it seems that people prefer to be ignorant than think about it."

Fear of reptiles has cropped up in some weird ways, he says. "There's cultures south of the border that are terrified of geckos. Because of their smooth translucent skin, they think they're like embryos, and, if a pregnant woman encounters a gecko she'll have a miscarriage.

"In Arizona, you need a hunting license to collect lizards, the same license as you need if you're hunting deer. The license restricts how many you can gather of different species and where you can collect them. Gila monsters have special protection; you need a special permit, which almost no one can get.

"People who keep lizards often decide eventually to release them back into the wild. Though they have good intentions, this isn't a good idea for several reasons. If you keep other animals the lizard may have picked up parasites or pathogens that it'll spread to the wild population. There may be a roadrunner waiting behind a rock to pick it off. If you don't let it go in the same exact spot you captured it, or if it's the wrong time of day or the wrong season, the likelihood of that animal surviving is nil.

"You might look at a little side-blotch lizard and say, 'Who gives a damn about this little animal?' But because they have such a high turnover, they feed a lot of animals. They eat insects and provide meat for other animals to utilize. A tiny lizard that seems so insignificant can be extremely important to energy utilization in a desert community. I usually dislike talking about 'balance of nature' because, it's always in a state of flux. I also try to keep people from thinking of themselves as some evil beast that's doing what no other animal would do. Any animal would do what we have done. It's biologically sensible to try and produce more of yourselves and utilize whatever resources are necessary to do it. People need to stop feeling guilty. A biologist I know likens our environment to an airplane wing. Yeah, you might be able take a number of rivets out of an airplane wing and get by, but once you remove a critical number, it's going down.

"I like what I see in our environment here, and I don't want it to change, I would ask people if they like what they see here. If you like it, but say, 'I don't like this or that,' well, it's all tied together. I believe this museum is important because it can give people an understanding of the desert. There's a lot of books out, but I think people would rather take in their knowledge by visiting a facility like this. It's a painless way to impart a lot of valuable information to people."

LAST LIZARD THOUGHT

Lizards seem to rank near the bottom of most people's lists of their favorite animals. Herpetologist Craig Ivani's suspicion that people have trouble relating to their "differentness" might explain why, but it might be more enlightened to see them as he does, filling critical roles in delicate eco-systems all over the planet. Lizards consume massive quantities of insects while serving as a food source for birds, mammals, and other reptiles. This in turn effects the other animals, which determines whole systems' ability to operate. It would be a far different world without them.

Though many people fear lizards like they do snakes, they're harmless to humans. In fact, with their amazing appetite for insects, many species are beneficial to people. Only the American Southwest's Gila monster and the Mexican beaded lizard are venomous. Human beings have found lizards useful as pets, insect-controlling guests, entertainment, sources of food and leather, medicinal cures, mythological beings, decorative accents on manufactured goods, and advertising icons.

Lizards' amazing adaptations, along with their incredible range of behaviors make them endlessly fascinating animals. I came away from my research with greatly increased respect and admiration, both for the creatures themselves, and for the many ways they have insinuated themselves into our cultures. If this book has done the same for you, dear reader, I consider it a success.

Top: *A rare shot of the perky predator, as Gila monsters prefer to hang out underground. This particular fella seems to like having his picture taken. He's quite the lil' poser! Sure he looks cute, but when he bites this jawboner clamps on like a pitbull. Bottom: No way this could have been faked. I mean, that's obviously a nicotine high bugging out the eyes of this puffin' predator. But at least the demon weed doesn't appear to have stunted his growth. On the contrary, judging by the size of the background shrubbery, he's grown to the size of a Buick LeSabre!*

SELECTED BIBLIOGRAPHY

African Folktales, selected and retold by Roger D. Abrahams,
    New York: Pantheon Books, 1983.

Ecology and Natural History of Desert Lizards, Eric R. Pianka,
    Princeton, NJ: Princeton University Press, 1986.

The Encyclopedia of Myths and Legends, Stuart Gordon,
    London: Headline Publishing, 1993.

Gila Monster, David E. Brown and Neil Carmony, Salt Lake
    City: The University of Utah Press, 1999.

Green Iguanas, John Coburn, Neptune City, NJ: T.F.H.
    Publications, Inc., 1994.

Horned Lizards, Jane Manaster, Austin, TX: University of Texas
    Press, 1997.

Komodo Dragon On Location, Kathy Darling, New York:
    Lothrop, Lee & Shepard Books, 1997.

Leonard Maltin's Movie and Video Guide 2000, edited by
    Leonard Maltin, New York: Plume, 1999.

The Masks of God: Primitive Mythology, Joseph Campbell,
    New York: The Penguin Group,1959.

Myths and Legends of the Polynesians, Johannes C. Andersen,
    New York: Dover Publications, 1995.

*National Audubon Society Pocket Guide: Familiar Reptiles &
    Amphibians of North America*, New York: Alfred A. Knopf,
    1988.

WHICH WAY TO VEGAS?, watercolor, by Tim Shields, 1996.

BUYER'S GUIDE

Our thanks to the following galleries and stores for providing the visuals for this book. Sources are listed alphabetically and include page numbers for the objects they refer to. In some cases both the manufacturer and retailer are listed. Some retailers are listed not because they sell a specific item included in this book, but because they are a great source for lizardabilia.

Accoutrements
P.O. Box 30811
Seattle, WA 98103
mcphee.com
various rubber lizards

Arizona Beach Company
The Arizona Center
455 North Third Street
Phoenix, AZ 85004
(602) 252-4744

Arizona Highways
The Arizona Center
455 North Third Street
Phoenix, AZ 85004
(602) 957-0381
night-light, page 3
thermometer, page 5
pewter pin, page 5

Arizona–Sonora Desert Museum
2021 North Kinney Road
Tucson, AZ 85743-8918
(520) 883-2702
www.desertmuseum.org

Club Earth
30 Martin Street, Unit 3B1
Cumberland, RI 02864
(401) 333-3090
hand puppets, page 8

Desert Gatherings
116 N. Roosevelt Avenue
Chandler, AZ 85226
(480)961-0715
wall sculpture, page 21

Geo Crafts
P.O. Box 297
Nanticoke, PA 18634
(570) 331-0800
doormat, page 1

Jayne's Marketplace
The Arizona Center
455 North Third Street
Phoenix, AZ 85016

Jutenhoops
Town and Country Shopping
Center
2103 East Camelback
Phoenix, AZ 85016
(602) 957-8006
rubber lizards, page vi
hand puppets, page 8
wall sculpture, page 21

Linens and Things
4701 North Twentieth Street
Phoenix, AZ 85016
(602)667-3000
doormat, page 1

Neon-Lithics
Spotlight Designs
205 West Benedict Street, #19
San Bernardino, CA 92408
(909) 885-5740
night-light, page 3

Oak Creek Canyon Designs
The Arizona Center
455 North Third Street
Phoenix, AZ 85004
(602) 253-3372

Qué Pasa
The Arizona Center
455 North Third Street
Phoenix, AZ 85004
(602) 253-6691
paper weight, page 1
folk art horned toad, page 2
wall sculpture, page 3

United Designs
P.O. Box 1200
Noble, OK 73068
(405) 257-6245
thermometer, page 5

APPENDIX

INDEX

Photo by Ed Mell.

ABOUT THE AUTHOR

Jim Cherry writes fact for magazines and fiction (so far) for himself. He studied English at the University of San Francisco before launching on a career in illustration. Eventually, he bought a computer to do graphics, which brought things full circle when he fooled around with a word processing program and became a writer, after all.

He lives and works in a historic, Phoenix neighborhood, with a small air fern to keep him company, about which, he asks, "what kinda companion is this? It's hard to tell if the thing's even alive!"